The Buildings of Georgian Whitby

The Buildings of Georgian Whitby

Andrew White

Ryburn Publishing
KEELE UNIVERSITY PRESS

First published in 1995
by Ryburn Publishing
an imprint of
Keele University Press
Keele, Staffordshire

© Andrew White
Composed by KUP
and printed by Hartnolls,
Bodmin, England
ISBN 185331 141 3

Contents

Acknowledgements

I would like to thank a number of people for their help and encouragement, in particular the successive Hon. Keepers and the Hon. Librarian of the Whitby Literary & Philosophical Society, Harold Brown, the staff of the Technical Services Dept. of Scarborough Borough Council, the Whitby Mission and the staff of the National Monuments Record in London. The superb library of the Society of Antiquaries has also been most useful. Finally, my family also deserves gratitude for putting up with my perpetual photography and note-taking on our visits to Whitby.

Picture Credits

Georgian Whitby

Whitby is a town unlike any other. It shares some of the common features of seaside resorts, of small ports and of fishing harbours, but it is all of these and none of these. It underwent its greatest period of prosperity between about 1700 and 1840 under the multiple influences of shipbuilding, shipowning, the hire of vessels as military transports, the Greenland whale-fishery and the coal trade, in all of which Whitby played a part out of all proportion to its size.[1] Although the town has grown markedly in area since then, it has increased very little in population. In the eighteenth century a population of ten to twelve thousand put it in the same league as many county towns; today such a population makes a small town. So, we must adjust our views of size and significance to take in the fact that two centuries ago Whitby was relatively much more important economically than it is today.

The piers and harbour entrance as they were in 1777, before large-scale harbour works took place, from a view by H. Chapman. (Courtesy of Whitby Lit. & Phil. Society)

Whitby's prosperity during the eighteenth century was in no small part due to the ownership of colliers such as this bark depicted on a tin-glazed bowl now in Liverpool Museum, inscribed 'Success to the Whitby 1772'.

The great changes experienced by the town during the eighteenth century are best expressed in a poem by the Whitby barber John Twisleton, quoted in the *Whitby Repository* for 1826:

A Poem in Praise of Whitby

by John Twisleton

What a place is Whitby grown!
Once but a poor fisher town,
Barren of trade, all callings dead,
A poor man scarce could get his bread.
For he was thought a man of note,
Who governed a fishing boat;
And though he gained a homely fare
By daily toil and constant care,
Would to the poor more kindness show,
Than some who have their thousands now.
Their houses then were very low,
The covering only made of straw,
Daub'd up with mortar, lime, and lath,
The outside white, the inside black –
But now, like Yarmouth, as its said
They've chang'd *white* herrings into *red*.

A water-colour drawing of Bagdale from the west, before the fall of the Abbey's great west window in 1794. The houses on the right have hardly changed but the Bagdale Beck running in front of them is now culverted. Near the left of the picture, the long low building is the Theatre in Scate Lane.

To Whitby's honour evermore
The pride of all our northern shore,
It was the war I say by which,
This place became so vastly rich;
For you may trust me, it is true,
One half the town is built quite new;
In famous houses, few excel...

...Nigh to the church, all such as list,
May go to hear the Methodist;
And if I be not told a lie,
A playhouse will be built hard by;
So as you choose, may spend your time,
In carnal pleasure or divine...

...Our transport ships by wind and tide,
Have made our masters swell with pride,
When little time before the war,
Their clothes were daub'd with pitch and tar;
In winter time to keep them warm
They'd put on stockings made of yarn:–
I say before the war beginning,
Would wear a coat of housewife spinning;
That if on board the ship you'd look,
Scarce knew the Captain from the Cook...

While no more than doggerel, this poem nicely catches the pretensions of the newly-rich middle class. The war referred to is almost certainly the Seven Years War (1756–63), in which the hiring of Whitby ships for transport purposes so signally changed the fortunes of the town.

The feature of Whitby which most strikes the eye is the uneven nature of the ground; houses rise up and slide down the steep cliffs, facing in all directions and producing a vast variety of intersecting planes.[2] It is hard to pick out individual buildings, and to some extent the whole seems more than the sum of its parts. However, once the eye has started to analyse detail, it is apparent that Whitby is the result of largely organic growth. As prosperity grew, the pressure for housing grew with it. Former gardens were built upon, giving rise to the characteristic pattern of yards and ginnels which are so common in the north of England. Most of these properties were let for rent and shared facilities such as privies, wells and drying grounds.

In the 1950s many of the most picturesque yards were demolished as slums, especially those in Church Street.[3] It is hard to believe such widespread destruction could take place so recently, especially as even at the time there was great public outcry. Those who lived in the yards no doubt appreciated the change, while there was some attempt to

Below and opposite are two views of the galleried houses in Boulby Bank, demolished in 1959. When we look beyond their picturesque qualities we see that they had a degree of uniformity suggesting that they were built at the same time by one landlord. The galleries gave access to the several tenements in each property.

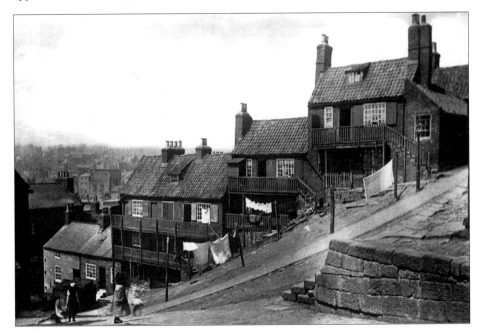

BOULBY BANK. WHITBY.

maintain the visual interest of the cliff-side position in the replacement buildings, laudable enough for its time. Many of the houses in yards which remained have now been sold to incomers as holiday cottages or private houses. Their visual charm is often as a group, to which individual buildings contribute, not as great architecture, but as something very out of the ordinary. It is hard (and wrong) to conceive of them being 'designed'; they represent natural and unplanned growth, although odd groups of houses within them may have some unifying feature.

Many of the streets as we see them today form encroachments upon the harbour. Grape Lane and Sandgate, along with the staithes on the other side of the harbour, originate in the piling and stiffening of the original sloping muddy banks. Once these encroachments had stabilized, houses, shops and whole streets were built upon them. Even then, many of the buildings had to be constructed upon piles themselves. The whole geography of the lower harbour was thus altered from the medieval period onwards, and the process still continues.

Whitby's greatest prosperity, based on the coal trade, the alum industry, shipbuilding and whaling, led not only to a great deal of rebuilding, but also to a large influx of people from the countryside requiring accommodation. Consequently, the predominant 'feel' and scale of Whitby is Georgian.

Wooler's chart of 1740, showing the approaches to Whitby by sea and a crude plan of the town itself. This is the earliest surviving plan of Whitby.

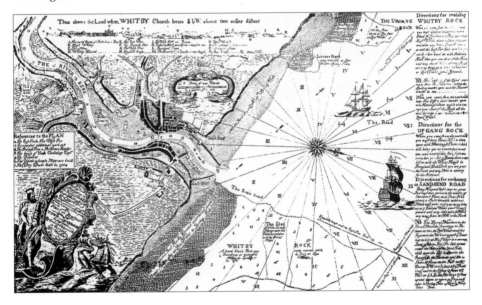

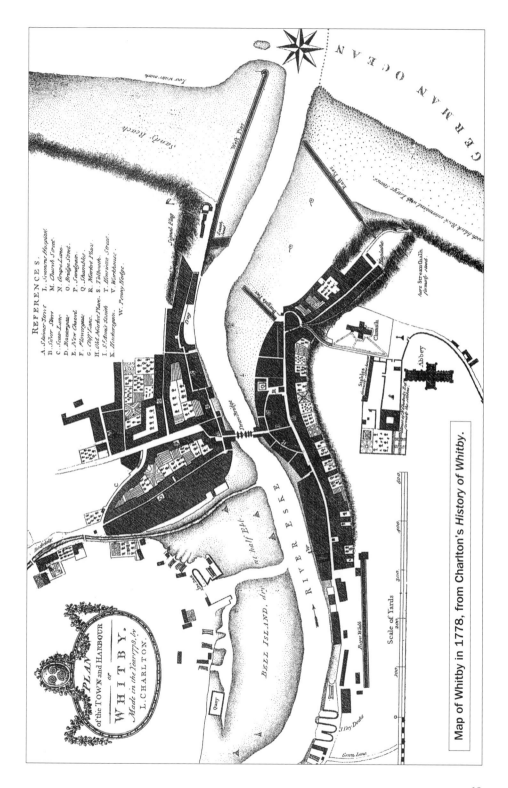

Map of Whitby in 1778, from Charlton's *History of Whitby*.

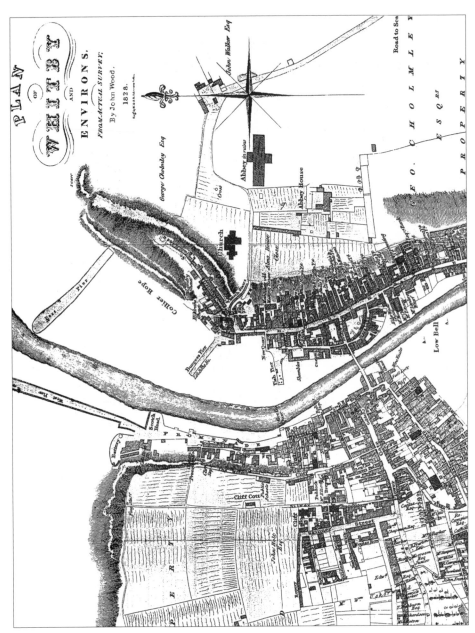

Part of John Wood's map of Whitby in 1828, the most detailed map of the town to appear before the work of the Ordnance Survey. It shows the densely-packed yards of Church Street and Baxtergate and the more spacious recent developments of New Buildings, Skinner Street and Well Close Square.

14

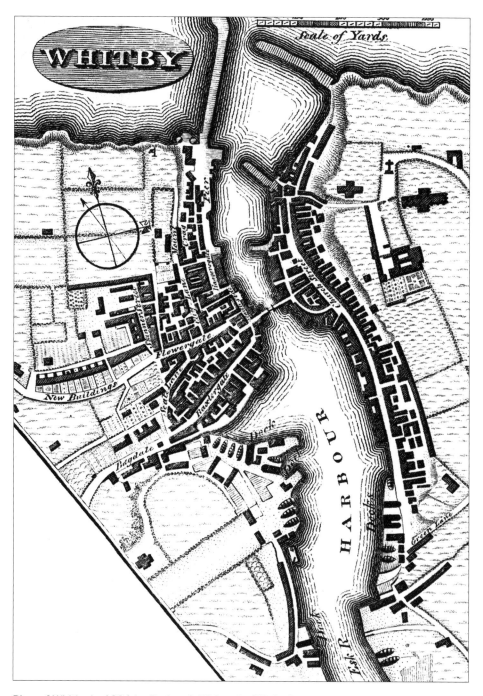

Plan of Whitby in 1824 by Barber & Whitwell of York, from Young's *A Picture of Whitby*.

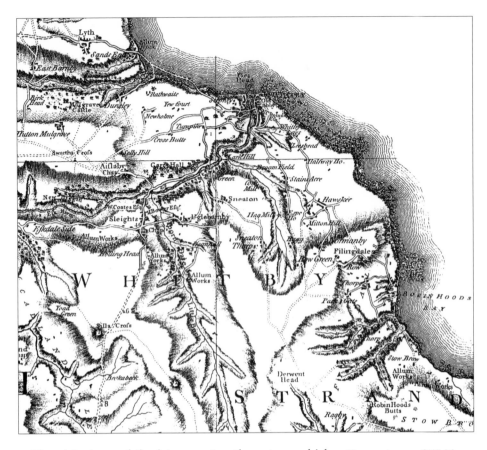

The environs of Whitby in the eighteenth century from Thomas Jeffrey's map of Yorkshire, 1775.

The plain town of the late seventeenth century, which had a high degree of social uniformity, supported by a dislike of 'show' inherent in its strongly Quaker and Nonconformist community, developed during the eighteenth century into a town of considerable diversity. A new successful middle class sought property in keeping with its aspirations, leading to the building of Whitby's two main Georgian terraces, while others, mainly landowners, started to build substantial houses on the outskirts of the town. Within the town, however, there was that lack of social stratification in houses that one comes to expect of Georgian towns outside the metropolis. Rich and poor lived side by side and areas which later were to be stigmatized as 'rough' in those days still held a number of 'respectable' inhabitants. Respectability by association was very largely a Victorian invention.

Apart from its rich heritage of buildings of this period, Whitby owes the origin of a number of institutions such as its library, museum and Literary & Philosophical Society to this era of intellectual endeavour, which in retrospect represents the high-water mark of the town's cultural life. Figures such as the two historians of Whitby, Lionel Charlton and Revd George Young, the artist John Bird and the Quaker dynasty of the Chapmans, were among the driving spirits behind the town's renaissance.

Much of Whitby's charm lies in the intricacy of its layout. One rapidly becomes aware that normal methods of studying the highly-compressed and interlocking building plots will not do. Frequently they simply defy analysis.

Building Materials

There is no single dominant building material in Whitby. Local stone of excellent quality was available close by, but so was brick brought by sea, and perhaps used as ballast by ships returning from the Thames and Humber. The exact source of the brick used in Whitby is unknown; probably there were many. T. S. Willan[4] records cargoes of bricks coming into Whitby from Hull in 1683–4 and in 1731, and there is no reason to believe that these were unusual. The source of some of these bricks may have been the south bank of the Humber, around Barton. In Charlton's day (the second half of the eighteenth century) there was a tilery at the northern end of Skinner Street, which perhaps supplied pantiles for the roofs, which are such a characteristic feature of Whitby. Before that, according to Charlton, tiles were brought by sea from Sunderland, Shields and elsewhere.[5] He also implies that bricks were made in Whitby, although the site of the brickyard is unknown. Brick is usually laid in Flemish Bond (alternating headers and stretchers in every course) but there are quite a large number of cases where English Garden Wall Bond (three courses of stretchers followed by a course of headers) and its variants are used.

There does not seem to have been much social distinction between brick and stone either. Well-built houses in both materials stand side by side in St Hilda's Terrace and Bagdale, the best addresses in Whitby, while large detached houses in the town and its outskirts are more or less equally divided between the two materials.

Certainly by far the oddest building material of this period is represented by the shed rediscovered and dismantled in 1930 not far from the gasworks on the west bank of the Esk.[6] It was of cruck construction, covered in canvas, but the crucks were not of wood; they were made up of whales' jawbones! This dates them to the latter half of the eighteenth century or to the first thirty or so years of the nineteenth century, when Whitby sent whalers up to the Arctic.

Stone Sources

One of Whitby's more significant exports, as well as a material in widespread local use, was stone for building. It came from the Lower Deltaic series and was in the form of a freely workable sandstone from the 'washout channels' in the delta of an ancient river. These channels had filled with sand which became a rock virtually devoid of bedding planes.[7] As well as being readily workable, this stone had the virtue of hardening as it weathered and of resisting the effects of immersion, so it was made use of in bridge and harbour works.

A remarkable photograph, taken in 1930 by Frank Sutcliffe, showing a cruck-built shed based on seven pairs of whale jawbones (some have already been removed) near the gasworks and the Scarborough railway viaduct. Since Whitby's involvement in the whaling trade came to an end in 1837, and the most prolific years were in the early nineteenth century, it is likely that the shed dated from then. (Courtesy of Hull City Museums)

This stone was used almost universally in Whitby, one of the rare exceptions being the late Georgian house at Airy Hill where a Carboniferous sandstone was brought from West Yorkshire, no doubt at great expense.[8] One wonders whether this was at the desire of the owner, or whether the architect came from that area and was accustomed to working with the local stone. The local sandstone was ashlared in several of the houses in Bagdale and St Hilda's Terrace but can also commonly be seen in walls and humbler buildings with the herringbone tooling so characteristic of the area. It weathers to a variety of colours, from buff to dark brown.

The main source for this Lower Deltaic sandstone was at Aislaby, three miles to the south-west. The quarry here no longer functions, but in its day its products were sent by sea from Whitby to build Margate and Ramsgate piers, the foundations of London and Waterloo bridges, Covent Garden Market and London Docks, to quote but a few examples. Houghton Hall, too, in Norfolk, was built of Aislaby stone in 1720, carried from Whitby to King's Lynn by sea. Whitby piers were built from the same stone, which was available in very large blocks. Some were absolutely huge. William Scoresby wrote of stones of 100 cubic feet or 6½ tons. In the building of the West Pier in 1814 a single stone of 12 tons was used.[9] The former quarries seam the moor to the south of the A171 and to the west of Aislaby church, at around NZ 850087.

Airy Hill from the south. An access road to the high level bridge now cuts across the former gardens.

Architects

Very few architects are known for Whitby buildings. Jonathan Pickernell, who designed the Town Hall in the Market Place, was the Harbour Engineer, and was responsible for the West Pier.[10] His grandson, Francis, designed the lighthouse at the end of that pier in 1831. Another Harbour Engineer, John Peacock, was responsible for the Commercial Newsroom in Haggersgate in 1813.[11]

John Bolton was responsible in 1826 for the combined Baths, Museum and Library building in Pier Road.[12] He appears in the Universal British Directory for 1798 as a stonemason, and Dr English records that he worked on the building of the West Pier. It was quite usual in Georgian times for a successful and competent stonemason or bricklayer to aspire to the title of architect, even if he had no formal training. Bolton may also have undertaken a number of speculative building works such as the houses in Prince's Place.

Mark Girouard has suggested that a number of high-quality houses in Whitby may be the work of Newcastle

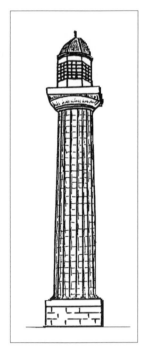

The West Pier lighthouse.

Prince's Place, off Spring Hill, consists of two rows of stone and brick houses respectively, set end to end.

The newly-opened Public Baths, Library and Museum in 1827, from an engraving in the *Whitby Magazine*.

architects, since they seem to have little in common with other Yorkshire buildings.[13] There was a strong trading and business link with the Tyne, while the difficulties of inland transport over the wild moors towards York meant that Whitby had less contact in this direction than one might imagine. There is a more than passing resemblance between several of the larger houses of Whitby, including features such as Gibbs' surrounds to ground-floor windows, 'layering' of the façade and unusual combinations of windows, which may prove on further research to be the signature of one particular architect. In so far as these are all elements in common use one should use great care in attributing on purely stylistic grounds.

John Carr of York may be responsible for one or two of the larger houses; he was so prolific and so well known in Yorkshire that it seems hardly possible that he failed to find any commissions there. Certainly, as Surveyor of Bridges for the North Riding he rebuilt the bridge over the Eastrow Beck at nearby Sandsend in 1777.[14] Such commissions often brought an architect to the attention of the local gentry and further commissions might flow from this.

William Hurst of Doncaster (1787–1844) designed Sneaton Castle in 1819 for Col. Wilson, MP for York, and also Sneaton church. His name was proposed as architect for the Baths, Museum and Library building in Pier Road in 1825,

but in the event he failed to win the commission, on the grounds that he lived too far away.[15] Carr and Hurst were connected by William Lindley, the pupil of the former and mentor to the latter. Lindley practised in Doncaster but had a large clientele among the gentry of Yorkshire and beyond. It may be his liking for recessed windows and a multiplicity of planes that we see in some of the larger Whitby houses, such as Airy Hill.[16]

Sneaton Castle from the north-east, from an engraving after John Bird, *c.1824*, in Young's *A Picture of Whitby.*

Among other known architects whose main practice lay elsewhere, Sir John Soane[17] and William Atkinson[18] both worked at Mulgrave Castle, in 1786 and 1805–16 respectively. Mulgrave was the home of Lord Mulgrave, whose connections were the most aristocratic in the district; his choice of architects represents a different level of patronage than most of those who had houses built in and around Whitby.

Masons and Craftsmen

We have already come across John Bolton, 'architect' of the combined Baths, Museum and Library building in 1826. A Trade Directory of 1798[19] records John Bolton, James Hutchinson and John Skinner as masons. Baines' Directory of 1823[20] has a much fuller list – it may not only be that numbers had grown but that the directory was more comprehensive. The list of masons under 'Stone & Marble

Mulgrave Castle from the south-east, from an engraving after John Bird, c.1824, in Young's *A Picture of Whitby*.

Mulgrave Castle from an engraving by W. Radclyffe after J. P. Neale, 1829.

Masons & Statuaries' (some of whom may have been bricklayers as well) includes Peter Appleton, John Bolton, Jane Close, William Fewster, Thomas Fortune, Thomas Overand (slate), Henry Robinson, Richard Stainthorp and William Tyerman. Jane Close may have been a widow who carried on her former husband's business. Certainly female masons were a great rarity.

Matthew Corner, 'builder', who died in 1803 aged 78, is commemorated by a gravestone in the churchyard of the Parish Church. He is worthy of further study, since the designation of 'builder' is rare before the Victorian period.

John Cappelman, mason, who died in 1779, left half a house called 'Ebenezer' in Henrietta Street and also a freehold estate in Church Street worth at least two hundred pounds.[21] This is probably to be identified with Cappelman's Yard, one of those yards demolished in the slum clearance of the late 1950s.

There were also in 1823 three tile merchants, two of whom also dealt in bricks; Edward Beaumont, John Bolton (again) and Gideon Smales, who is known to have had a hand in many businesses, such as shipbuilding and repairing. He also appears in the list of carpenters.

Usually, carpenters played an almost equal part in building, sometimes going into partnership with masons. However, in Whitby it is difficult to distinguish house carpenters from ship's carpenters and shipbuilders. This was a distinction which they would have found difficult to make themselves. Perhaps they worked on houses when there was a lull in the ship-building or repairing trade and vice versa. Baines' Directory of 1823 lists no less than fifteen firms of 'Carpenters – House and Ship' but fails to differentiate them. Carpenters played a larger part in Georgian house-building than we tend to assume. Houses of brick or stone often included substantial timbers within their walls to support, level and tie the structure together, as well as the roofing, flooring, staircases and panelling which we would expect.[22]

Style and Design

Much of what we recognize as typically Georgian in buildings is provided by a combination of elegant proportions, good materials and a range of simple details. At its simplest the Whitby brick terraced house is very close to those being built in London between the Great Fire and the 1720s, with radiused relieving arches over the doors and windows and motifs like a shallow projecting string course between storeys. Good examples may be seen in Henrietta Street, dating to no earlier than about 1760. Others can be found in Church Street, Flowergate, Baxtergate, and in many of the yards.

Of course many houses are much more complex and make use of a wide range of motifs, such as a variety of planes to break up what would otherwise be rather dull areas of stonework. Such devices can be seen on larger houses such as Airy Hill or Larpool Hall. Some frontages can become positively busy when a number of motifs are used in the same façade, such as at Haggersgate House.

Brick is usually laid in one of two bonds, as we have seen. Stone is almost always ashlared, with very narrow joints. A plain appearance was often the aim, with just enough detail in window and door surrounds, together perhaps with a contrasting colour on brickwork such as white paint to articulate the whole. We will examine doors and windows shortly.

Henrietta Street, looking north. This street was built in 1761 on a ledge of the cliff at the north end of Church Street and was briefly fashionable until the instability of the subsoil brought many houses crashing down in 1787.

Proportion is not just a matter of mathematics, although there were guidelines in many of the pattern books to suggest how large windows should be, based on the capacity of the room they were to light, and what the relative sizes should be of window openings and of the masonry piers between.[23] Often it was just a matter of what seemed right, and undeniably many local builders who were not particularly well-educated or well-versed in theory managed to hit on the right proportions by experience and by natural taste.

Although many buildings have classically-inspired details such as columns and capitals to their door-cases, there are relatively few buildings in Whitby which are straightforward essays in classical style. Jonathan Pickernell's Town Hall of 1788 and Francis Pickernell's Lighthouse of 1831 are about as close as any come to it. One reason is the relative lack of new churches – St Ninian's was built in a sort of basic brick Gothick, while the Parish Church used an imitation of the Early English lancet style, but with the lancets filled with very domestic-looking clear glass. The great church-building phase in Whitby, because the old parish guarded its privileges so tightly, was not until the mid-nineteenth century. Another reason is the absence of almshouses in Whitby – or at least of groups of them – until the Seamen's

Haggersgate House, now the Whitby Mission.

Hospital was built. Almshouses were frequently built by a private benefactor to a new style, and elsewhere introduced new ideas of classical architecture, on a small scale, to many a town.

Doors and Windows

Many of the houses have doorcases which are straight from the pages of eighteenth century builders' pattern books, such as that of 19 Well Close Square.[24] Others have a distinct 'feel' of Whitby and may have been worked up by local builders on their own. The houses in Brunswick Terrace have very distinctive fanlights; that at 10 Brunswick Street, although sadly neglected at the time of writing, is probably the finest in Whitby. Where there are fanlights, the capitals are often elongated and the entablature broken in order to fit the window under a columned canopy. Many fanlights are in fact dummies, made from a wooden panel with tracery laid over it.

Some of the larger houses have elaborate windows or surrounds. Haggersgate House has so-called 'Gibbs' surrounds to the ground floor windows, as does Airy Hill. The uppermost group of three houses in Bagdale Terrace has extremely ornamental carved leaf-trail surrounds to some of its first-floor windows, which seems an exceedingly old-fashioned and baroque feature for 1816.

The Parish Church. On the left is the medieval north transept and on the right the northern extension to the nave, built in 1819. A serious attempt has been made to match the style of the earlier work, including the use of lancet windows.

Former doorway, with Tuscan doorcase, of the George Hotel in Baxtergate.

Tuscan doorcase of 23 Baxtergate.

An extraordinarily tall Tuscan doorcase at the Black Swan, 69 Baxtergate.

Adam-style recessed doorcase at 21 St Hilda's Terrace.

Doorcase with fluted pilasters at 19 Well Close Square.

Ionic doorcase at 4 St Hilda's Terrace.

Paired Ionic doorcases with dummy fanlights over at Brunswick Terrace.

Ionic pilasters frame this doorcase at
1 Brunswick Street.

Elaborate fanlight at 27 Skinner Street.

Tuscan doorcase and
honeysuckle fanlight at
10 Brunswick Street.

Venetian windows, consisting of a round-headed centre framed by two square-headed lights, are fairly common, particularly to light staircases. Flowergate House has a so-called 'Diocletian' window, named after the great blank elliptical openings on the Baths of Diocletian in Rome. This design is uncommon in Whitby, though elsewhere it is often the device used to break up blank pediments. In Whitby some houses have a round window or else a plaster roundel in this position, performing the same function.

Most common of all features is the very long stair window, seen at its most exaggerated in the great house in Grape Lane called Green Gate. The device itself is eminently sensible and is a very common borrowing into polite architecture from the vernacular tradition in the north of England.

Services

It is difficult to generalize about the servicing of Whitby houses. The great majority of them are quite modest and although servants were employed, to our eyes, surprisingly low down on the social scale, they may in many cases have lived in close contact with their employers. The tradition of sharing and communal activity was still very strong and survived until Victorian times, when demands for greater segregation of employers and servants became general. Quaker households in particular tended to avoid excessive social distinctions at all times.

Nonetheless, there is evidence in larger houses such as those at the lower end of St Hilda's Terrace of both basements and garrets, presumably with concomitant servants' halls. In these larger houses, maidservants probably lived in the garrets while menservants occupied lofts over stables and coach-houses, relatively few of which have survived intact. There are a few remaining in Back St Hilda's Terrace. Before details from censuses became available from 1841 onwards, there is little information about the number and type of servants employed, but one interesting piece of evidence comes from Young's analysis of population in about 1815.[25] The great disproportion of males to females (37:92) in the twenty-four families of New Buildings (as St Hilda's Terrace was originally known) is due, he says, to the number of female servants in that street, which also gives some indication of the size of the (largely) invisible servant population. In London a few years later female servants are believed to have made up one in fifteen of the total population.

Although hardly to be described as servants in our sense of the word, many seagoing apprentices would have spent the winter ashore while their ships were laid up, occupying attics and such-like spaces in their masters' houses. They were meant to study or make themselves generally useful. Large numbers had to be accommodated, because the whalers did not leave until spring while the colliers had a winter recess to avoid the worst of the storms. A late seventeenth-century house in Grape Lane, now the Captain Cook Memorial Museum, serves as an example of a once-common arrangement. James Cook, while apprenticed to Capt. Walker in the 1750s, was unusual in spending his spare time in study while wintering in his master's house. Not unnaturally he made himself a firm favourite with Walker's housekeeper, who was unable to treat him with appropriate awe when he returned, years later, as a celebrity.[26]

Gardens and Summer-Houses

Although there is no satisfactory contemporary map of eighteenth-century Whitby (Charlton's is merely a block plan) and Wood's otherwise excellent map of 1828 is not very detailed in this respect, an examination of the 1852 60" Ordnance Survey reveals the presence of many summer-houses, especially on the slopes facing south-east above Bagdale. It is in this area that Whitby's two main Georgian terraces stand, and almost certainly the summer-houses are associated with these. Their date cannot easily be ascertained because they do not survive but it is most likely that they are contemporary, or nearly so, with these terraces. Work on the town of Kendal[27] has shown how many houses possessed summer-houses, either within their immediate grounds or else upon some detached pleasure ground nearby, and the popularity of such structures in Georgian times is becoming clear. High Stakesby Manor had no less than two gazebos of brick in its garden, dating from the mid-eighteenth century.

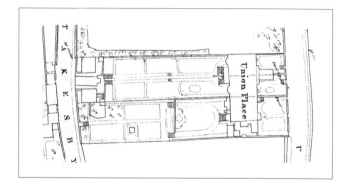

Block plan showing the houses and gardens of Union Place, Upgang Road, based on the 1852 OS 60" map. It is clear from the layout that the main entrance was always at the back (Upgang Road, seen here on the right) leaving the garden side very private.

The pressure upon space imposed by the burgeoning growth of the town in the eighteenth century meant that gardens were something of a luxury. Larger houses on the fringes of the town such as Airy Hill, Meadowfields and Field House met with no difficulties in this direction and each of them had large gardens, virtually all now built over. In the older core of the town, gardens were unusual and many earlier open spaces at the rear, whether they were yards or gardens as such, were mostly converted to cheaper rented housing during the eighteenth century. The fine stone house at 23 Baxtergate is something of an exception, and still retains its garden, with access partly below ground level from the front.

It was those two large developments of New Buildings (St Hilda's Terrace) and Bagdale that sported the largest and best gardens. In New Buildings not only did they lie in front

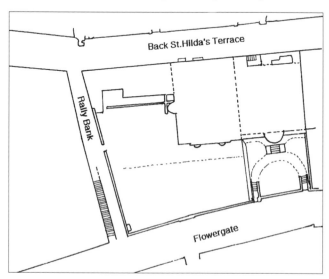

Block plan of nos. 21 and 22 St Hilda's Terrace based on the 1852 OS 60" map.

33

of the houses, giving some privacy from the street, but also behind, separated by a service road giving access in many cases to coach-houses. Some of the larger houses also had detached portions opposite, in the area now covered by Pannett Park. We cannot really tell how they were planted, but those front gardens of the terrace in Bagdale, now rather dank and shrubby, are almost certainly due to subsequent Victorian taste. In their original form they probably had a much more open aspect, with gravelled walks and low planting, including borders. Lawns were not typical of Georgian town houses, nor were elaborate flower beds or specimen trees.[28]

Poorer Houses

Rich and poor in Whitby lived close together, and many of the streets can show grand and modest houses standing side by side. The poorest section of the community, however, was to be found in the burgeoning yards which lay behind the street frontages, where small cottages and tenements had been built on former gardens. These yards varied greatly in the quality of their buildings and in their salubriousness – or lack of it. Linskill Square, off Baxtergate, is relatively wide and airy and its houses show a degree of uniformity; some of this is due to recent tidying, but by no means all. At the other end of the scale some yards are very cramped and lacking in both light and air. In the days before mains drainage they must have been unspeakable.

Long, typically medieval, plots – which are usually called 'burgage plots' even if in Whitby there were in strict legal fact no burgesses to enjoy them – ran back to the cliffs and down to the river. In time the open ground at the rear of these plots became built up, often when frontage owners started to capitalize on their assets. They built and rented out cheap cottages and tenements to the newcomers who were attracted by prosperity, and so we find so-called 'yards' developing behind the main street frontages.

Many of these houses have gone, and others are either so altered or so basic in their detailing that it is hard to put any date on them. Quite a large proportion, however, seems to exhibit some small detail, such as an attractive porch, a well-proportioned sash window, or good brickwork, which have cumulative value.

Many poorer houses exhibit a large amount of structural timber, especially in external gallery access and stairs. The best examples of these have now gone, but old pictures of Boulby Bank, Cappelman's Yard, or Barry's Square, show just how prevalent the use of timber was. Boulby Bank, though one of the most picturesque areas of Whitby, displayed in its paired doors opening off galleries a surprising degree of regularity, and it must have been conceived and built in one go – a far cry from the unplanned and organic growth of many yards.

Of course relatively few of the poor would have lived in newly-built houses. Most would have lived in the decaying and sub-divided houses of an earlier period and would in any case have shared many facilities, such as wells, privies and drying-grounds. It was commonplace for widows or bachelors to rent a couple of rooms in a shared house, even if they were not particularly poor, and many families did likewise, hence the complex stairs and galleries giving access to upper floors of shared buildings, mentioned above.

There was also a large body of transients in Whitby, unmarried sailors and the like, who had little need of a permanent home. Many of the poorer householders would have been glad to rent such men a room for a few weeks or months between voyages, in return for a little much-needed cash. Probate inventories for the period show many such men, owning little but the clothes on their backs.[29]

Public Buildings

Since Whitby was not a borough, but had been first in the pocket of the Abbey and later in that of the Cholmley family, it lacked the range of public buildings often associated with this status. However, it gained a set of Improvement Commissioners, from Acts of Parliament of 1764 and 1789,[30] and to an extent they served the function of a Town Council.

In the Market Place is the so-called Town Hall, built in 1788 in the classical style by Jonathan Pickernell, Harbour Engineer and builder of the West Pier, for Mr Nathaniel Cholmley, the lord of the manor. It is a very simple but effective building, with a single large meeting-room on the first floor, carried on Tuscan colonnades, and approached by a spiral staircase in a central drum.

The Town Hall.

Another prominent building which now no longer serves its original purpose is the former Baths, Museum and Library building, completed in 1827.[31] It stands in Pier Road and is a plain but well-proportioned structure of three storeys and seven bays – the oriel at either end is a later addition.

The Whitby Commercial Newsroom, built in 1813, is a charming narrow little building on Marine Parade, now the home of 'The Dracula Experience'. The Articles of Agreement for its construction have been used to reveal how it was built and what it looked like when new.[32]

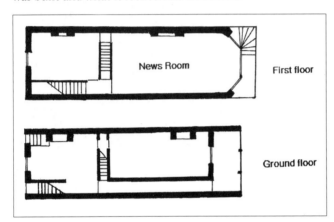

Floor-plan of the Commercial Newsroom, Haggersgate, after G. Leach and the 1852 OS 60" map.

Churches

Since the Middle Ages, Whitby had been one huge parish with a few chapels of ease. One of these chapels was that of St Ninian in Baxtergate. Rebuilt on a new site this was to be the first new church in Whitby for several centuries and the precursor of a number of others. Since it was built from the subscriptions of its congregation it was also a so-called 'proprietary church'. It is a plain brick structure with pointed windows, approached by a domestic-type door with its hood carried on brackets, up a double flight of steps from Baxtergate. In its original form it had an apsidal chancel and galleries around three sides internally, with a small square bell-turret on the roof; the latter was removed about thirty years ago. Re-pewing of the nave and extensive alterations to the chancel took place in 1881–2, under the guidance of a very high-church priest. The galleries, however, retain a number of original box-pews.[33] The main frontage carries an elementary pediment.

Interior view at gallery level of St Ninian's Church, Baxtergate. Although the nave and chancel owe their appearance to remodelling of the 1880s the gallery still conveys the original feeling of the Georgian church.

The Parish Church of St Mary is the work of many different centuries but the Georgian period saw it greatly extended and altogether altered in its internal appearance. Like most ancient churches it reflects the changes in the community which uses it. In this case that community grew significantly in size and wealth during the eighteenth century and the long narrow Norman church was no longer capable of housing it. Enlargements to the fabric and the amazing proliferation of galleries were moves to accommodate the growing number of parishioners but ultimately the monopolistic hold of the Parish Church over its huge parish had to be broken. This did not happen until the mid-nineteenth century, with the building of new churches, although St Ninian's Church had done something to ease the situation in the 1770s.

St Mary's 'nearly preserved its ancient form till about the year 1744, when the north wall growing very bad, and being in danger of falling, it was taken down and rebuilt, with the windows in somewhat a more modern taste' according to Charlton.[34] We cannot judge how 'modern' this was, for it was once more demolished in 1819 in order to build a large new north aisle between the nave and north transept. Internally there is no distinction between transept and aisle.

Externally the aisle is very plain, lit by five tall lancets containing intersecting tracery, and obviously intended to match the thirteenth-century north transept.

Much of the fenestration of the church was filled with clear glass at this time or earlier in the Georgian period. The lancet windows were mostly retained but the windows of the south transept are of a square domestic type with intersecting tracery and add considerable charm to the external appearance of the church. All this was naturally anathema to the Victorians – the Revd William Keane described it in 1863 as '... now perhaps the most depraved

The Parish Church from the south-east, showing steps leading up to the galleries in the south transept and sky-lights in the roof providing light for them.

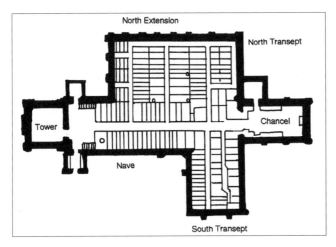

Left and facing page: Plans of the Parish Church, showing the positions of box pews and galleries at the fullest extent by about 1819.

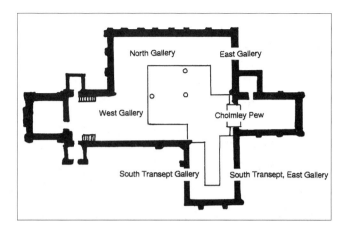

sacred building in the kingdom'(!)[35] – but with commend-
able and rare restraint they refrained from filling the
windows with stained glass or from reordering the interior.
Restoration did not take place until 1905 and by great good
fortune was placed in the hands of W. D. Caroë, whose work
was limited in scope and tasteful.[36]

It is the galleries which give the interior its special
character. No less than six were fitted into the church
between 1697 and 1819, filling both transepts, the north
and south sides, and with no less than two at the west end.
By 1819, it is said, the church could accommodate two and
a half thousand people.

All the other churches (of the Church of England that is)
had to wait until the nineteenth century. A pleasing vision
of what Whitby might have become, had it continued its
Georgian growth, is contained in the *Whitby Magazine*
for 1827, where there is an imaginary description of the
town in 1913.[37]

There were a number of good plain Nonconformist
chapels and meeting houses, such as the Presbyterian
Chapel in Flowergate and the Friends' Meeting House in
Church Street, both in their present form dating from the
early nineteenth century, and many others that have gone,
including all of the various eighteenth-century Methodist
chapels. The first of these stood in Henrietta Street and
was short-lived, collapsing with other buildings there in the
late 1780s. Its successor stood at the upper end of Church
Street. Wesley himself preached there while the chapel was
still unfinished; men were stationed along the frontless
galleries to stop others falling over the edge! Wesley thought

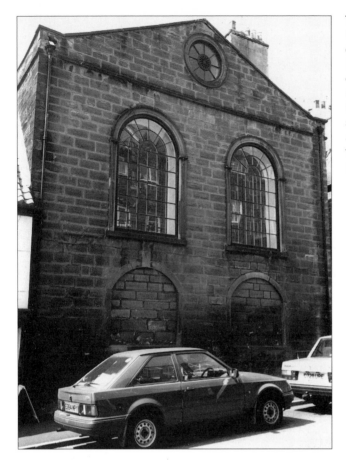

The Friends' Meeting House in Church Street, dating from 1813. In Whitby, the Society of Friends or Quakers numbered most of the influential merchants, shipowners and bankers among its members in the eighteenth and early nineteenth centuries.

it one of the most beautiful chapels in the country.[38] The Methodist movement was plagued by secession and most of the breakaway groups established their own chapels, such as the Primitive Methodists or Ranters who built their meeting-house in a yard lower down Church Street.

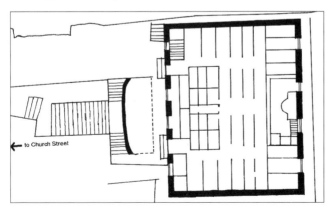

to Church Street

Plan of the Methodist Chapel in Church Street, built in 1788. It was approached by several flights of steps and when built was hemmed in by houses, later demolished. John Wesley himself preached here.

An anonymous lithograph showing the West Pier, complete with its new lighthouse, shortly after 1831. Note the bollards, capstans and rubbing-strip on the eastern side, all concerned with the warping-in of sailing ships.

Harbour Works

It is not surprising that a town such as Whitby which relied almost entirely on its maritime trade should have undertaken substantial harbour works. It employed three resident Harbour Engineers; Jonathan Pickernell from 1781 to 1812, James Peacock from 1812 to 1822, and Francis Pickernell for almost forty years from 1822.[39] Francis was the grandson of Jonathan Pickernell; Jonathan's son was Harbour Engineer at Sunderland.

But the story begins much earlier. In 1702, Whitby, as a port of refuge on the dangerous east coast, was fortunate in obtaining an Act of Parliament which allowed it to charge passing tolls on all ships, except for those of Yarmouth. This right was continued by various succeeding Acts and was only extinguished in 1861.[40] The income allowed the building of harbour facilities and piers to provide some protection against the seas, which on its own the town could never have done.

This work went on for more than a century and a half, transforming the nature and fortunes of Whitby. With the exception of the two lighthouses, the end of the East Pier, and the two extensions, the shape of the harbour as we know it is entirely a result of Georgian industry. The list of structures built or rebuilt in this period is impressive: most of the two main East and West Piers, Tate Hill Pier, the Fish Pier, the Scotch Head, various staithes and the bridge, which linked the two halves of the town at a natural narrowing of the harbour. This was rebuilt as a drawbridge in 1766 to designs by Robert Shout of Helmsley[41] and replaced by a swivel bridge in 1835. A wider swivel bridge replaced this in turn in 1908. The lighthouse on the West Pier, dating from 1831, is a splendid fluted Greek Doric column, combining beauty with utility.[42] Although technically just not Georgian in date it is Georgian in style and inspiration. The Pilotage in Pier Road was also the work of Francis Pickernell. Along with the harbour works went the establishment of gun batteries to protect the shipping lying in the harbour or in Whitby Roads. Some traces of these remain.

This engraving by Finden after W. Westall, published in 1829, shows the old drawbridge, built in 1766 by Robert Shout of Helmsley and soon to be replaced by a swing bridge. The way in which harbourside structures were built out on timber piles can clearly be seen.

New Developments

Whitby saw five major new developments during the eighteenth and early nineteenth centuries, apart from several minor ones. The first of these was the building of Henrietta Street on a ledge of the cliff known previously as the Haggerlyth, beyond the Church Stairs, in about 1761. For a brief period this became a fashionable area but a series of landslides caused by movement of the unstable boulder clays on which it stood made its popularity wane by the 1780s.[43]

Next came Farndale Fields, to the north of Flowergate, acquired by the Skinner brothers, William and John, for the sum of fifteen hundred pounds in 1762. This resulted in the building of Skinner Street, Well Close Square, Routh Walk and perhaps Poplar Row.[44] This development was highly thought of at the time, because of its 'regularity', but later shop fronts have obscured most of the original buildings.

Even in the mid-eighteenth century Bagdale was called 'near Whitby'. The valley of the Bagdale Beck was sparsely inhabited and waiting for the tentacles of development to follow the main road out of Whitby to the south-west. In about 1780 work started on the terrace of sixteen houses lining its northern side. These were not to a uniform design but were grouped in twos and threes. A service road (Walker Street) gave access to their backs while long gardens ran down to Bagdale at the front. Further gardens extended backwards between Walker Street and Newton Street, belonging to the Bagdale houses, and two houses here and a short terrace on the corner of Newton Street and Brunswick Street (now Brunswick Terrace) were probably thought of at the time as being part of the same development. The building of Bagdale Terrace may have taken some time. Young notes in addenda to his *History of Whitby* that 'three elegant houses have been added to Bagdale by Mr Michael Teasdale'. This reference, which must date from *c*.1816, seems to relate to nos. 12–14, the stone houses at the upper end of the terrace.[45]

St Hilda's Terrace, or New Buildings, was begun a few years earlier. No. 14 has a datestone of 1779 on its rear wall. This terrace of twenty-five houses exhibits considerable variation in size and style. Most of the larger houses are at the eastern end; the last four or so to the west are quite a lot smaller. As late as about 1816 'a splendid house has been erected by Edward Chapman, Esq. in the vacant space in the middle of the New Buildings'.[46] This was the Stone House, no. 21, which now forms Council Offices.

These developments provided some of the 'best addresses' in Whitby and the early occupiers included ship-owners, surgeons, gentlemen and their widows, as can be seen from Wood's map and early Directories (see Table 1 on page 46).

These two terraces had the advantage of a southerly aspect and an attractive view out over the harbour from steeply rising ground on the edge of the Bagdale valley, a position not unlike that of some Bath terraces.

The last large development to be considered is that at the western end of Bagdale, known in 1828 as Campion Ville, where Robert Campion built a villa and a row of cottages to go with his spinning mill and sailcloth factory. This, being

Nos. 21 and 22 St Hilda's Terrace. The upper floor of no. 22 has been added later. Because of the steep slope of the garden it has an entrance at basement level. No. 21 was built in 1816 for Edward Chapman and exhibits a number of Adam features, influenced by the new fashion for Grecian architecture.

Prospect Row, at the foot of Green Lane and close to Spital Bridge. Although by no means uniform in style these houses have matching dummy fanlights.

A narrow flight of steps gives access to the 1816 terraces of Prospect Place, established on ledges in the cliff.

an industrial settlement, does not fall into the same category as the previous four but is nonetheless of considerable interest.[47] More information can be found in the Gazetteer below.

Prospect Place, two parallel rows of stone houses up a flight of steps above Church Street, was built in 1816 by Gideon Smales. Early maps show three rows, not two. Although not in the same league as Bagdale or St Hilda's Terrace it was still 'respectable' as is born out by its complement of Master Mariners and the like among its first inhabitants. The same can be said for Prospect Row, at the foot of Green Lane, a small and probably unfinished development, and Prince's Place, off Spring Hill.[48]

Apart from these relatively small-scale pieces of urban planning most of Whitby's Georgian building took place within its old established streets and represents rebuilding or at least refronting of its older housing stock.

Table 1

Bagdale 1828		St Hilda's Terrace 1828	
	(From West)		(From West)
	(Friends' Burial Ground)	1	(Clark) Revd George Young
12	Mr Teasdale	2	Eliz. Moss, gentlewoman
13	Mr Scoresby	3	Mrs D. Cockerill,
14	William Jamieson		gentlewoman
15	Mr Featherson	4	John G. Loy MD, surgeon
16	Francis Agar, shipowner	5	Brewster
17	William Usherwood,	6	Brown
	shipowner	7	Thos. Marwood, shipowner
18	John Wardell, attorney	8	Hannah Hunter, gentlewoman
19	John Frankland Esq.	9	Israel Hunter, gent
	(Union Road)	10	Brown
20	Robert Usherwood,	11	George Langborne, shipowner
	shipowner	12	Martha Harrison,
21	William Willis, gent		gentlewoman
22	Thos. Simpson,	13	William Harrison, gent
	shipowner	14	Eliz. Harrison, gentlewoman
23	William Gibson, gent	15	William Middleton, gent
24	(Catholic Chapel)	16	Margaret Richardson,
	Revd George Haydock		shipowner
		17	Thos. Fishburn Esq.
		18	Barker
		19	Miss Margaret Presswick
		20	William Usherwood
			(Rally Bank)
		21	Edw. Chapman Esq.
		22	Rich. Moorsom Esq. Jun.,
			shipowner
		23	? R. Preston Esq.
		24	Mrs Ann Barker, gentlewoman
		25	William Chapman Esq.,
			shipowner

Sources: Wood's Map 1828 and Directories

Gazetteer

This is necessarily selective but includes the best and most accessible Georgian buildings in Whitby and its environs. There are many more, however, in private yards or which otherwise involve problems of access. May I emphasize that mention in this gazetteer does not imply any right of access. The privacy of the modern occupants should be preserved.

Former or alternative names are bracketed. If the whole entry is in brackets, the building no longer exists.

THE TOWN CENTRE

Bagdale

9 (Leesholme)   Stone, of three bays x three storeys, plus attic and basement. Door in end elevation. Prominent quoins at corners. The house is set somewhat below the present level of Bagdale and reflects the position of the now culverted Bagdale Beck. A drawing of 1794 in Whitby Museum (see page 9) shows that this house is virtually unchanged on the outside.

The Old Brewery   Brick with white stuccoed quoins and dressings, assymetrical. Two bays x two storeys to the left of the door, which has a small plain portico, and one bay to the right x three storeys and larger windows. A blocked door at the extreme right. The explanation seems to be that there was originally a wing which extended backwards at the right.

Bagdale Terrace   Sixteen houses to approximately the same building line, with long gardens in front and an access road behind. There is no single design but houses are grouped in ones, twos and threes within the terrace, which is further divided into two by Union Steps. This terrace was started soon after St Hilda's Terrace and belongs to the final two decades of the eighteenth century.

12–14 Three houses in one, built by Michael Teasdale in about 1816 (i.e. long after the rest).[49] Stone, of three x three bays x three storeys, plus attic and basement. The doors are set in bays three, six and nine, and have Corinthian columns and fanlights to the doorcases. The first floor windows over these doors have carved leaf-trail surrounds. The eaves carry balustrades and urns. At the rear, opposite the front doors, are long round-headed stair windows extending from the ground to first floors.

15–16 Pair, in brick, of four bays x two storeys, plus attic and basement. No. 16 has a box eaves cornice. Paired doors to centre with rectangular fanlights over.

17–18 Pair, in brick, of four bays x three storeys, plus attic and basement. Doorways paired to centre with fan-lights over. At the rear are long stair windows extending from the first to the second floor.

19 Brick, of five bays x two storeys plus attic and base-ment. Doorcase at centre with fluted pilasters and fanlight over. At the rear is a Venetian window lighting the stairs at first-floor level.

20–21 Pair, in stone, made to look like a single house. (The door of no. 20 opens at the side on to Union Steps).

Engraving of 'Whitby from the South-West', taken from a drawing by John Bird, which shows Bagdale Terrace in the foreground. In the background the houses of St Hilda's Terrace culminate in John Addison's mansion at the corner of Skinner Street.

Five bays x three storeys, plus attic and basement. Centrally placed door with fanlight and porch on fluted Doric columns. At the rear round-headed windows light the second floor and a ground floor extension.

22–23   Pair, in brick, of four bays x three storeys, plus attic and basement. The two outer bays are canted for their full height. The doors are paired at the centre, that of no. 23 with a doorcase and fanlight, and no. 22 with a later porch.

24   Brick, of five bays x two storeys, plus basement. Central doorway with later porch and fanlight. At the rear a Venetian window lights the stairs at first-floor level.

25–26   Pair, in brick, of six bays x two storeys, plus attic and basement. Paired doors at the centre with fanlights over.

27   Now the Catholic Presbytery. Stone, of three bays x two storeys, plus attic and basement. Pointed gable to centre front. The original Catholic church stood immediately behind.

Baxtergate

23   Probably built by the successful ship-builder Benjamin Coates[50] in the 1740s, this stone house is one of the most attractive in Whitby. The main entrance is up a few stairs, while a passage at ground level gives access to gardens at the rear. Stone, of four bays x three storeys, plus basement. Tuscan doorcase with fanlight. The original iron railings survive.

32   Brick with stone dressings, of four bays x four storeys and a modern shopfront. The second bay of windows is blank all the way up.

39–41   Brick, with variegated headers and stretchers. Prominent string courses and quoins, and an end elevation to Victoria Square of two bays. The last building was shortened and butchered in the 1960s to extend the roadway.

44–5   A pair of stone houses of two bays each x two storeys, with dormers in the steep roof and the doorways paired at the centre, with fanlights over.

48   Brick, of five bays x three storeys.

69 (The Black Swan)   Brick, of four bays x three storeys. The plain Tuscan doorcase is quite monumental in its proportions.

Linskill Square   On the east side there are several attractive brick cottages in English Garden Wall Bond with relieving arches over the windows.

The George Hotel   Brick, of four bays x three storeys, plus attic and basement. One window on the first floor is picked out for special treatment. A once-fine building, the home of the Holt family, its main frontage was to Baxtergate before Victoria Square and Station Square were created. The Georgian part now forms the rear and is sadly mutilated. Original ground-floor arrangements have been muddled up but the openings have stone dressings and the doorcase has Tuscan columns.

Opposite: No. 23 Baxtergate, the house of the shipowner Benjamin Coates. Unusually, it has managed to retain its original iron railings to the area and steps.

Below: Nos. 44 and 45 Baxtergate.

St Ninian's Church A proprietary church (owned by the thirty original proprietors and their successors) built in 1778 to supplement the Parish Church for the growing population on the west side of the town. It replaced an older, medieval, chapel of St Ninian on another site. Brick, on a stone base, with three pointed windows and a round window in the pediment in its street elevation and access via two sets of steps. Inside three galleries and a shallow apsidal chancel. Also, originally, a square cupola on the roof, removed some thirty years ago, because of dry rot.[51] The interior was extensively altered in the 1880s to provide for high Anglican liturgy but the galleries still give a feel of its eighteenth-century appearance.

Brunswick Street

10 Brick, of five bays x three storeys. In the centre is a doorcase with Tuscan columns and an exceptionally attractive honeysuckle fanlight. A Venetian window at the rear. At the time of writing this fine house is shamefully neglected. The interior is much institutionalized.

1–3 Brunswick Terrace Variegated brickwork, six bays x three storeys. The main doors are at first-floor level, approached by winding stairs, and have Ionic columns and dentillated pediments. A street at the back gives access to the main floor at apparent ground floor level, because of the sharp fall of the land. Each house has a long stair window at the rear.

(*Theatre* Built 1784, burnt down in 1823 and never replaced. It stood in the area of Newton Street and was a tall building. No evidence survives of its plan. Brunswick Terrace stands near its site).

Church Street

From Bridge Street to the foot of the Church Stairs there are many stretches of continuous Georgian buildings, albeit with modern shopfronts. The lower, southern, part of the street suffered badly in the demolitions of the late 1950s

Title-page of the play 'Streanshall Abbey' by the local playwright Francis Gibson, performed at the theatre in Scate Lane (now Brunswick Street) in 1799.

STREANSHALL ABBEY:

OR, THE

DANISH INVASION.

A PLAY OF FIVE ACTS:

As firſt performed at

The THEATRE in WHITBY,

Dec. 2d. 1799.

WRITTEN BY FRANCIS GIBSON, ESQ:

Ex noto fiĉtum carmen sequar. HOR.

Whitby,

PRINTED BY THOMAS WEBSTER.

Sold by G. G. and J. Robinſon, Paternoſter-Row, London.

1800.

and early 1960s. In the process all the old buildings on the riverward side were demolished along with many of those running up to the cliff on the east. This part of the street was widened at the same time.

11   Brick, in Flemish Bond, of two bays x three storeys, with a central doorway and stone quoins.

13 Scoresby House   Brick, in Flemish Bond, of two bays x three storeys. Over the door is painted the date '1760'.

No. 11 Church Street.

19–20   Brick cottages of two bays x two storeys each, with a prominent string course.

31 (Ship Inn Flats)   Brick, of three bays x three storeys.

37a (Abbeville Cottage)   Rendered, of one bay x two storeys, plus attic. Typical of the more modest Georgian cottages of Whitby, which are mostly to be found in yards and not, like this, on the street frontage.

44 (Boulby Bank)   Brick, rendered, of three bays x three storeys.

46   Stone house and shop, next to the Seamen's Hospital, the shop marked 'L. Paylor. Marine Store Dealer'. The shop has its own door, window and side passage, with tripartite windows above. The house has plain sashes, the door with a dummy fanlight over. An unusual survival and, because it has stood empty for several years, no doubt a fragile one.

51   Brick, of four bays x two storeys, plus basement. Pronounced string courses beneath the windows. The round-headed outer doorway with a fanlight is rather awkwardly contrived at the extreme right of the façade between ground and basement levels, indicating internal steps. Used *c.* 1800 as the bank of Robert and Margaret Campion, but internal detailing suggests it may be an earlier building.[52]

86 (Cook's Galley)   Brick, of four bays x four storeys.

88 (The Whitby Bookshop)   Rendered, of three bays x three storeys. It has a very slender suspended staircase in a central well.

96   Brick, of three bays x three storeys. It is a refronting of an older house with panelling and with mullioned windows to the rear.

105   Brick, of two bays x three storeys.

Middle Earth Tavern   Rendered, of five bays x two storeys, plus attic. The south wing is a formerly separate brick house of three storeys.

St Patrick's RC Church   Of brick in Flemish Bond. Six bays x two storeys on either side of a central passage giving access to Catholic School Yard. Originally a private house. The eaves have been raised later.

Rigden Cottage   Where Church Street turns up to the foot of the Church Stairs. Brick, of three bays x two storeys, plus basement. A through passage at ground floor level gives access to the rear.

Friends' Meeting House   Rebuilding of 1813 on an earlier site, in stone, with its end elevation to the street. Two round-headed windows over two blank openings at this end, and a circular window in the gable. As Pevsner rightly points out,[53] it is 'a little less humble' than many other Quaker meeting-houses. Increasing wealth among the Quaker community and controversy over the arming of ships by some Quaker shipowners were to cause a falling-off from the asceticism of the earlier Whitby community, which had been typified by Capt. Walker, James Cook's master.

Prospect Place   Two parallel rows (early maps all show three rows) of three-storey stone houses running along the

No. 51 Church Street, at one time the bank of Robert and Margaret Campion. The windows are like those of Poplar Row, while the fanlight, if original, is extraordinarily art nouveau in concept.

behind Victorian and later accretions. It most probably dates from soon after 1761, when Skinner Street was laid out. Stone, of five bays x three storeys, plus attic and basement to Flowergate, and a five-bay side elevation to Skinner Street. Ground-floor windows have Gibbs surrounds, first-floor windows are alternately pediment-headed and straight-headed. At second-floor level is a Diocletian window with a circular window above it. The central three bays are brought forward slightly and pedimented, while the door has its own, broken, pediment. There is balustrading at first-floor and eaves level. The side elevation is plainer, with a recessed Venetian window.[55]

Virtually all of this description should be in the past tense, since in the later nineteenth century the house became the Crown Hotel, involving alteration of much of the side elevation, raising of the eaves, and the building of shops with a sun lounge over in front of the main façade where the front garden used to be. Indeed, it is only by stepping back to the far side of Flowergate that one can see the traces of this building's splendid origins.

St Hilda's Terrace (also known originally as New Buildings or King Street)   Whitby's premier Georgian terrace, begun soon after 1778 (it does not appear on Charlton's map of 1778 but no. 14 has a datestone of 1779 on the rear). No. 25 shares the same building line but is part of the Farndale Fields development and so earlier than the rest. Perhaps its building suggested the idea of a terrace of superior houses.

The houses vary greatly in size, those at the western end being the smallest, and are a mixture of singles and pairs. No. 21 is of stone and later than the rest, dating from about 1816,[56] the remainder is of brick. The terrace is split by Rally Bank, between nos. 20 and 21. Long gardens run down to the road at the front while the backs of the houses are reached by a service road (Back St Hilda's Terrace). Behind this are further gardens, now in many cases in separate ownership, but a number of former coach-houses survive along the roadway.

According to the 1852 OS map many of the houses enjoyed summer-houses within their gardens or upon adjacent open land. There is little trace of these now. Many of the larger houses have been subdivided into flats.

1–2   Pair, in brick, of six bays x two storeys, plus attic. Paired doorcases with fluted pilasters to centre, with fanlights over. No. 2 has a stone coach-house opposite its back.

3–4   Pair, in brick, of six bays x two storeys, plus attic and basement. Centre four bays are brought forward under a pediment, in the middle of which is a plaster oval floral plaque. Dentillated cornice. Paired wooden Ionic pilastered doorcases to centre with fanlights over. Both houses have coach-houses opposite their backs.

5–6   Pair, in brick, but both subsequently altered, of six bays x two storeys, plus attic and basement. No. 6 has a wooden box eaves cornice and no. 5 a lower roof line. Opposite the back of no. 5 is a stone coach-house.

7–8   Pair, in brick, of six bays x two storeys, plus attic and basement. Paired plain doorways to centre (no. 7 has a fanlight over).

9–10   Pair, in brick, of six bays x two storeys, plus attic and basement. Both have plain doors set to the right of the respective façade. No. 10 has a canted stone bay replacing the original lower pair of windows.

11–12   Pair, in brick, of six bays x two storeys, plus attic and basement. Doorcase to left of each half, with Doric columns and fanlight over. No. 12 has a large later bow in place of two ground-floor windows. No. 11 has a stone coach-house opposite its back.

13–14   Pair, in brick, made to look like a single house. Five bays x two storeys, plus attic and basement. Steeply pitched pantiled roof with circular brick chimney stacks. Centrally placed doorway with Corinthian columns and fanlight over. The rear elevation carries a pair of plaques; that on no. 13 is blank but that on no. 14 reads 'H/CE/ 1779', perhaps for Christopher Harrison, shipowner, and his wife Elizabeth.

15–16   Pair, in pale brick. Five bays x three storeys, plus attic and basement. Central three bays brought forward

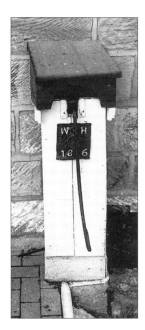

Pump inscribed 'W H 1816' in the former service yard at the rear of 15–16 St Hilda's Terrace, probably originally providing water for horses.

and pedimented with a circular window at the top. Two pilasters define the projecting bays between the first and second floor. A stone porch on three (!) columns with Ionic capitals serves both houses. Fanlights over doors. Half-round bay to rear of no. 16 with coach-house opposite. Also on this side of the service road is a pump with 'W H 1816' on its front.

17 Brick, of five bays x three storeys, plus attic and basement. Three bay projecting centre with pediment containing a round window. Dentillated cornice above first floor and string course running between and under second floor windows. Four pilasters dividing bays, becoming two at first floor level. An elaborate doorcase is covered by a later porch. At the rear is a fancy stone porch with a ground floor gallery to the left. A Venetian window at first floor level lights the stairs.

18–19 Pair, in brick, of five bays x three storeys. A central doorcase provides access to paired doors with pointed fanlights over. At the rear of both were 'bottle' windows lighting the stairs at first and second-floor level, but that of no. 18 is now obscured by the brick rear wing.

20 Brick, of three bays x two storeys. Two later canted bays replace the ground-floor windows. The door is placed centrally in a timber doorcase with a fanlight over. A stone coach house stands opposite the rear.

21 Known as 'The Stone House' and separated from no. 20 by Rally Bank. The main approach is from the rear, via a sunken doorway with Doric columns and a fanlight over, or from the west side via a similar doorway. This type of door is a common late Georgian motif, originating in Dublin but popularized by the Adam brothers in London.[57] Stone, of five bays x two storeys, the front framed by giant Doric pilasters. There are two two-bay stone extensions to the left. Inside is an attractive well staircase with an oval roof light. The hall has Ionic columns.

22 Brick, of five bays x three storeys, the ground floor rendered. The attic storey is a later addition, and does

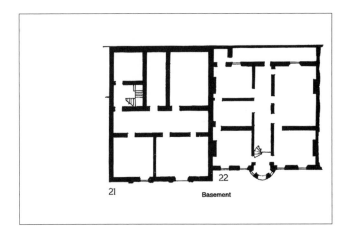

21   22   Basement

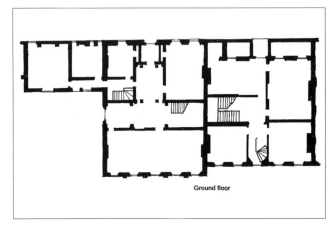

Ground floor

Plans of nos. 21 and 22 St Hilda's Terrace, based on plans kindly lent by Scarborough Borough Council Technical Services Department, with obvious later accretions removed. Because of the steep fall of the front garden the main front entrance to no. 22 is at basement level.

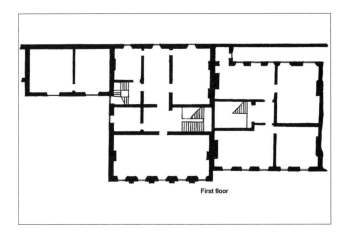

First floor

not match. Semi-circular projecting porch with railed balcony on columns. The centre window at first-floor level is larger. Half round window to light stairs at rear. The staircase also has a recessed oval roof light. The hall has an arch carried on Ionic columns. Stuccoed coach house opposite rear.

23 Brick (Flemish Bond) of five bays x two storeys, plus basement. Later attic storey. The centre three bays are brought forward and pedimented, the centre window of the pediment being a replacement for an original *œuil-de-bœuf*. Central doorway with fanlight and Doric columns. Dentillated cornices.

24 Brick, of five bays x two storeys, plus attics with dormers which are not original. Central doorway with columns. Dentillated cornice. Venetian window lighting stairs to rear.

25 (Lynden Gate) Although this appears to be part of the St Hilda's Terrace group it is in fact somewhat earlier than the rest, being built by William and John Skinner in 1762 – in other words it belongs to the Farndale Fields development.[58] Brick, of five bays x two storeys, plus attic and basement, with two extensions of one bay and three bays to the west. Central door with fanlight and porch on brackets. The extensions are now a separate property with access from the rear. The rear of the main house has a Venetian window at first-floor level lighting the stair.

Grape Lane

18–19 (Green Gate) Once the house and bank of Simpson, Chapman & Co., and long known by this name.[59] The original bank safe, concealed as an ordinary door, still survives at first floor level. Brick, of three bays x four storeys, plus a basement. Doorway at either side. Ground floor rusticated in stone or stucco. There are giant fluted wooden pilasters to each side, while at the rear is a huge long stair window containing no less than sixty panes of glass. On the flat roof is an octagonal 'Chinese lantern' of glass, also lighting the stairs. The whole building is unusually lofty for Whitby and towers above its humbler neighbours.

20–21   Pair, in brick, of four bays x two storeys, divided rather arbitrarily. On the left is a nice door with fanlight over.

Green Lane

2–4 (Prospect Row)   Three cottages of stone at the bottom of the hill, with blank fanlights over doors.

Haggersgate

The Whitby Mission (formerly Haggersgate House)   This was built for John Yeoman, a prominent shipowner, in about 1760.[60] Brick, with stone dressings, cornice and quoins, of five bays x three storeys. All the ground floor openings have Gibbs surrounds and there is a Tuscan portico. The pediment contains a circular window. Very grand, but in a curiously constricted position. It is sometimes claimed that the house originally stood alone and was abandoned by its owners when the area became built up, but deeds of surrounding houses show that the area was in fact built up from at least the seventeenth century. The interior is sadly very much institutionalized but retains some elaborate plaster cornices while the stair window, a partially blocked Venetian window, is framed in plaster foliage and has the remains of Ionic pilasters.

'The Dracula Experience'   For many years a photographers' studio but built in 1813 as Whitby Commercial Newsroom, on a very awkward narrow site, essentially of one bay's width, running through from Marine Parade to Haggersgate. It was built on deep piles into the sand and silt of the harbour. There is a fine round-headed window on the first floor of the rear elevation. The roof carries a very small cupola.[61]

15   Brick, of two bays x three storeys.

16   Brick, of five bays x three storeys, flanked by house door and passage door. It has prominent string courses and Gibbs surrounds to doors and windows.

17–18   Brick, with attractive doors.

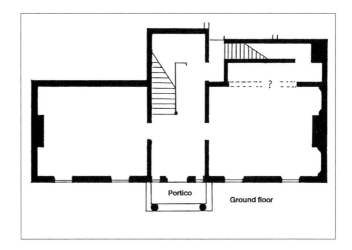

Portico   Ground floor

Haggersgate House, redrawn from plans kindly lent by the Whitby Mission. Some of the internal divisions are conjectural.

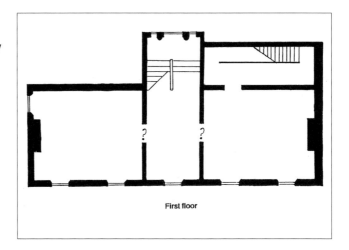

First floor

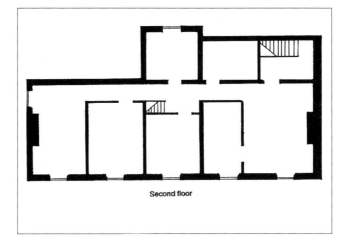

Second floor

The Star Inn, in Haggersgate, is typical of 1760s buildings in Whitby with its paired windows and prominent keystones.

Star Inn Stone, covered in stucco, of six bays x three storeys. Prominent keystones to windows, several of which are blocked. The extreme right hand bay is built over an arch giving access to Bakehouse Yard, one of those break-neck lanes running steeply down from the West Cliff which add so much to the charm of Whitby.

Henrietta Street

Laid out in 1761, and named after the lady of the manor. Built upon unstable alum shale and boulder clay it quickly proved a disaster, and in 1787 a great part of the street collapsed into the harbour, followed by another collapse in 1870 and others more recently. The southern end of the street survives, but the northern end, the Haggerlyth, remains empty. The most northerly houses show evidence of the instability of the subsoil, and the Spa Ladder, giving access to the East Pier, regularly needs to be extended as the cliff erodes.

6–10   Brick, with relieving arches over windows.

23–27   Brick, with relieving arches over windows.

Market Place

Town Hall   Stone, built in 1788 by Jonathan Pickernell, Harbour Engineer and builder of the West Pier, for Mr Nathaniel Cholmley, lord of the manor. It is a very simple but effective building, with a single large room on the first floor, carried on Tuscan tetrastyle colonnades surrounding a central drum containing a spiral stair. The upper room was originally used for the manor court and later by the Improvement Commissioners. A cupola on the roof carries the clock and bell.[62]

The Town Hall and Market-Place from an engraving by Green, c. 1816, in Young's *A Picture of Whitby.*

Marine Parade

The Old Jet Works   Stone, of three bays x three storeys. The ground floor has modern shop windows but the first floor has a central round-headed window.

Whitby Fashion House   Perhaps originally a sailcloth factory. Stone, of six bays and four storeys, with anomalous doors at first floor level. The windows are much smaller than most domestic ones.

Pier Road

Pier Inn   Two buildings of two bays x four storeys and two bays x three storeys, both rendered.

The Battery   Although the block of buildings now forming the Khyber Pass Restaurant is somewhat later, the curved gun battery itself and the two circular stores or magazines at each end, with conical roofs, are shown on Jonathan Pickernell's plan of the harbour works in 1796 and in a painting of the same date.[63] They seem to be an unusual survival. This gun battery and another at the end of the West Pier were designed to protect shipping lying in Whitby Roads. Another battery, on the Haggerlyth, protected the harbour itself, but has long since fallen over the cliff. Whitby shipping frequently fell prey to privateers during the American War of Independence and during the Napoleonic War.

Magpie Café Formerly this seems to have been the Pilotage, where pilots awaited the demand for their services in bringing ships into and out of the port. There were twelve pilots under a master in 1823.[64] Three bays x three storeys,

One of the two roundhouses which form part of the Battery at the foot of the West Pier, perhaps originally stores or magazines. They can be seen in Capt. Thornhill's view of 1796 (opposite).

with the main entrance at first-floor level, perhaps because of the progressive raising of the staithe. Tripartite windows on the second floor and large projecting bows at either end of the first floor. It was designed by Francis Pickernell.

Harbour Diner (formerly Baths, Museum and Library)
Stone, of seven bays x three storeys. The upper oriel windows are not original. The centre three bays were designed to look like a private house, with a rusticated ground floor and a centrally placed front door. Two giant pilasters frame this section, beyond which the matching end pairs of bays were of three and two storeys respectively, with a smaller doorway at each end. This threefold division expresses the three functions of the building, which were, however, separated horizontally. The ground floor is now wholly altered. John Bolton was the architect – he is recorded as 'stone mason' in 1798 – and the building was opened in 1827. It is of interest to learn that Mr Hurst of Doncaster was first proposed as architect for this building, perhaps on the initiative of Col. Wilson of Sneaton Castle, who had employed him some years earlier, but that it was felt he lived too far away to supervize the job.[65]

There are many other attractive Georgian buildings here, their frontages now disguised by the impedimenta of seaside amusements.

Poplar Row (behind Skinner Street)

Two pairs of tall houses in variegated brick, each of two bays x three storeys, plus basement. Steps to front door. Windows consist on each floor of a single and a pair, i.e. two windows under one lintel. This pairing of narrow windows is fairly frequent in Whitby. These houses were probably built as part of the Skinner brothers' Farndale Fields development after 1762, along with parts of Well Close Square and Routh Walk.

Prince's Place

A terrace of cottages, some of stone and some of brick, opening off Spring Hill. This area was developed in the latter

Poplar Row, tucked behind Skinner Street, is part of the Farndale Fields development by the Skinner brothers. Its lack of a cornice and the high parapet give a somewhat spartan appearance.

part of the eighteenth century and became a 'respectable' place to live. Wood's map of 1828 shows 'Bolton's mason yd.' just below it, so perhaps John Bolton was responsible for the development of this and King Place (now Victoria Place).

Ropery House

An important brick house, of five bays x three storeys, the centre projecting slightly. At the rear are two projecting wings in English Garden Wall Bond. Between the wings is a Venetian window.

Routh Walk

1–4 Two pairs of modest brick houses, each of two bays x two storeys, with a basement. The windows have prominent keystones.

St Hilda's Terrace see Flowergate

Sandgate

The feel of this street is predominantly pre-Georgian.

Silver Street

Quarterdeck Antiques Brick, of three bays x two storeys, the brick laid in alternating headers and stretchers of contrasting colours. Dentillated cornice. Doorcase has fluted pilasters and blank fanlight.

12–13 Brick, of five bays x two storeys, plus basement. Doors paired at centre.

22–23 Brick, of three bays each x two storeys, plus basement. Doorways paired at centre.

(Former Congregational Hall) Stone, with diamond broaching, of six bays x two storeys. A now-illegible plaque occupies the centre of the eastern elevation.

18 Brick, of six bays x two storeys. Door in centre. Prominent quoins. The side wall is in stone.

Skinner Street

This formed part of the Farndale Fields development of 1762 by the Skinner brothers which began the colonization of the West Cliff. Originally the street was a cul-de-sac, closed off at its northern end by a ropewalk. It is apparent that it took a long time for houses to be built along it since sixteen years later Lionel Charlton was still looking forward to when it should be complete and '... soon exceed all the other streets in Whitby, both for beauty and magnificence'[66]. One looks in vain today for these qualities in Skinner Street.

(Lynden Gate) see **Flowergate**

29–33 Brick, ground floors replaced by shop fronts. Nothing special, but along with nos. 5 and 9, all that is left of Georgian Skinner Street.

Spital Bridge

Former factory Nine bays x three storeys. The two upper storeys are in brick, on a stone base.

Spring Hill

Spring Cottage (formerly Ings Cottage) Stone, of three bays x two storeys, with a Tuscan doorcase approached by steps.

(Formerly Spring Hill House Now covered by the Hospital site this house was once known as 'Lobster Hall', because it was built by the guard of the Whitby–York coach from the profits of carrying lobsters. Later it formed the Nurses' Home. Stone, of five bays, with a three-bay centre framed by giant pilasters, and a Tuscan porch.[67])

Stakesby Vale

(Former Spinning Mill)   Stone, built in 1807 and extended in 1814 by Robert Campion, who was also a banker, as a sailcloth factory. Subsequently it has had many other uses, such as a sweet factory and a carpet warehouse. Its reuse has removed most of the evidence of its original function, but the original fireproofing and iron columns survive.

Union Steps

The Haven   Brick front with stone dressings, of four bays x two storeys, plus attic. All other walls of stone, diamond broached. A single-storey extension to the right has a projecting canted bay. Built before 1812. One wonders whether this is the first of a failed terrace, intended to occupy the hillslope between Bagdale and St Hilda's Terrace.

Upgang Lane

7–11 (formerly Union Place, after the Union Mill which stood nearby)   Stranded among later housing these tall

Spring Cottage, Spring Hill, is rather grander than its name would suggest.

houses face away from Upgang Lane. Their northern elevations carry very long stair windows like that in Grape Lane (q.v.), though not as extreme. No. 7 is stone, of four bays x three storeys, nos. 9–11 are brick, of five bays x three storeys, the two outermost bays being canted.

Victoria Place (formerly King Place)

Two houses with brick fronts and stone sides seem to be all that was ever built of this small development, just below Prince's Place and perhaps of the same date. On the OS 60" map of 1852 it looks as though a whole terrace had been intended. They are approached by steps over a high stone basement.

Victoria Square (formerly Bagdale Terrace)

4, 6 & 8   Three similar modest houses in brick, a single and a pair. Each of two bays x two storeys. Unusual tripartite windows with prominent keystones, matched by the smaller windows and doors. Most have suffered the loss of their glazing bars. No. 4 has a fanlight and fluted pilasters to the door.

(*Former Central Restaurant*   Demolished to make way for the Bus Station this long plain brick house, of five bays x two storeys, plus a two-bay extension at the left-hand end

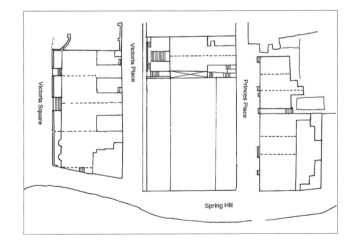

Block plan of Victoria Square, Victoria Place and Prince's Place, based on the 1852 OS 60" map. It looks from this as though Victoria Place was meant to extend as far as Spring Hill.

(perhaps originally the office) was the home first of Thomas Hutchinson and then of the Barrys, ship-builders. Like Whitehall and Esk House this was built to overlook the shipyard. Later it became the station-master's house for the nearby railway station.[68])

Victoria Place (formerly King Place) consists of only two houses and seems to represent an unfinished terrace.

Well Close Square

This was part of the Farndale Fields development of 1762 but, like Skinner Street, has little to show of its origins today.

5 Facing away from the street. The rear elevation has a long stair window of twenty lights and was once longer still.

19 Rendered, of four bays x two storeys. Superb doorcase with fluted pilasters and fanlight over.

Tanshelf Brick, of three bays x three storeys, set back from the street, with the door to the left. The doorcase has Doric columns. Built in 1789, according to a sale catalogue. Tall and narrow, the very epitome of a Georgian town-house. It nonetheless looks as if it was intended to be part of a terrace,

Facing Page: 'Tanshelf', Well Close Square, is the perfect embodiment of a Georgian town-house, and could well be the model for many a dolls' house, with its clean lines and tall narrow frontage.

which is possible since the pompous Edwardian house immediately to its east (formerly the Harold Private Hotel) seems to occupy the sites of two Georgian houses and has, rather incongruously, a Georgian doorcase, perhaps a relic of its predecessor.

OUTLYING BUILDINGS

Airy Hill

Stone, but not the local Aislaby stone. Instead a darker
Carboniferous sandstone was brought all the way from West
Yorkshire to build this house of the Moorsom family in
c.1790.[69] The main part is of five bays x two storeys plus attic
and basement, with wings. The lower windows have Gibbs'
surrounds and Ionic pilasters articulate the three bay
pedimented centre on both main elevations. On the north
side is a curious 'broken' porch, partly Victorian, carried on
Tuscan columns with a Venetian window above. When first
built the house stood a good way out of Whitby, with views
over the town. Time has dealt unkindly with it and now a
busy road to the high level bridge cuts across the former
gardens.

Bog Hall Tannery

Stone domestic buildings survive alongside the road known
as Bog Hall, but there are no other remnants of the former
large tannery, which in 1828 belonged to Mr Cook.[70]

The weigh-house at Bog
Hall when relatively new,
from an engraving in
Young's *A Picture of
Whitby.*

Bog Hall Weigh-House

Built in 1835 for the Whitby & Pickering Railway, this very early piece of railway architecture deserves better than to be allowed to fall apart through neglect. It should be consolidated while there is still something left to consolidate. What is left is the flat front facing the track, with a large window opening. It is in beautifully cut ashlar masonry with fine joints. Part of the curving side walls also survives.[71]

(Bog Hall

In 1930 a canvas covered shed beside the railway line near the gasworks was demolished and found to be carried upon seven pairs of whale-jawbones, used like cruck-frames, quite the most remarkable vernacular use of available materials![72])

Carr Hall, Ruswarp

Stone, set high above the road overlooking the Esk between Ruswarp and Sleights. Five bays x two storeys, with a canted centre bay.

The last remains of the original 1835 weigh-house at Bog Hall, an exceptionally early piece of railway architecture and deserving of restoration.

(Esk House

Destroyed by a bomb in World War Two, its site is now
covered by Council housing. Just one gatepost survives.
This was the house of Thomas Fishburn, ship-builder and,
typically, overlooked his shipyard.[73])

(Field House, Upgang Lane

Stone, of three bays x two storeys, sideways on to the road.
The two outer bays were canted for their full height.
Pediment over centre and projecting Tuscan tetrastyle
porch with steps at either side. Fanlight over. The house,
after standing empty and in decay for some years, was finally
demolished c.1959.[74])

Larpool Hall, Hawsker

Stone, of five bays x three storeys, with two wings of two
bays x two storeys each. The centre bay is brought forward
slightly and pedimented. Pairs of deep string courses mark
out the storey division. The porch and canted bay to the left
hand wing are later additions. Now a country house hotel.

(Meadowfield

Built of brick in the early nineteenth century this house
survived little more than a century before being demolished. Its site is now occupied by post-war housing. It had
a central block of five bays x two storeys and wings of three
bays each. It appears in an engraving by John Bird.[75])

(The Mount

A house associated with the Whitehall shipyard and long
in the ownership of the Turnbull family. Its site is now
occupied by inter-war housing.)

Block plan of Meadowfield House, based on the 1852 OS 60" map.

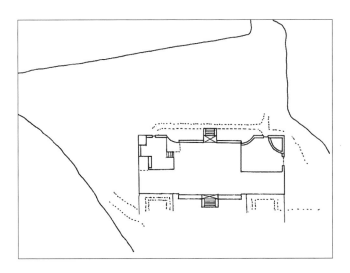

Mulgrave Castle, Lythe

The house of the Rt. Hon. Earl Mulgrave in a prominent position to the west of Sandsend and set in very extensive parkland, which includes its medieval predecessors, a motte and bailey and part of a stone castle. It has a complex building history. A much older core – Mulgrave Hall – was extended by John Soane in 1786–7 and then the whole was gothicized as Mulgrave Castle and further extended by William Atkinson between 1805 and 1814. The windows, however, remain domestic Georgian.[76]

Newton House, Ugglebarnby

Stone, with a three-bay centre and two-bay projecting wings. Associated with this house is an obelisk recording the taming of previous wild moorland by its owner, Jonas Brown, to make pleasure grounds and a curious shelter known as 'the Hermitage', dated 1790 and contrived out of a huge rock, quite close to the waterfall of Falling Foss.

Ruswarp Mill

Brick, Flemish Bond, of five bays x three storeys, with stone dressings and cornice. A tablet on the façade reads: 'These mills were erected at the expence of Natha. Cholmley Esq.

by Philip Williams Engineer 1752'. Several serious fires have removed traces of the original layout but the façade is very fine.

Sneaton Castle

Stone, in a theatrically-Gothic castellated style with corner turrets and a high curtain wall around the gardens, built in 1819 for Col. Wilson, MP for York, by William Hurst of Doncaster.[77] The main façade is of five bays x two storeys, with a central doorcase, flanked by two three-storey corner towers. The windows are conventionally Georgian.

High Stakesby Manor House

Stone, of three bays with a central Greek Doric porch to the side elevation. Early nineteenth century. The house is hemmed in by modern developments but was once on the edge of the country and isolated.

Lower Stakesby Manor

Brick, of five bays x two storeys, plus attic and basement. The centre three bays are brought forward and pedimented, with a Venetian doorcase at the centre. The rear elevation has a single-bay projection with a Venetian window on the first floor. Like High Stakesby it is now surrounded by modern houses which have crept into the former gardens.

North elevation of Lower Stakesby Manor House. The house once stood in its own grounds among the fields but the grounds have now been invaded by suburban housing.

Whitehall

Standing above, and with a view over the shipyard of the same name, which is now derelict and in a sorry state. Stuccoed, three bays x two storeys. Door at the centre with porch on fluted Doric columns, the two end bays canted for their full height.

Lower Stakesby Manor, south front.

Woodlands, Aislaby

Stone, of five bays x three x two storeys, plus attic and basement. Prominent quoins and crenellated parapets. Built for Henry Yeoman, a prominent alum-works owner.[78]

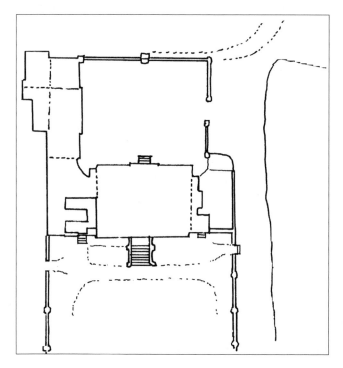

Block plan of Lower Stakesby Manor House, based on the 1852 OS 60" map.

Notes

1   A. White, *A History of Whitby* (1993).

2   G. H. J. Daysh (ed.), *A Survey of Whitby and its Surrounding Area* (1958).

3   A. T. Pile, *Buildings of Old Whitby* (1979).

4   T. S. Willan, *The English Coasting Trade 1600–1750* (1938), 118, 120.

5   L. Charlton, *The History of Whitby and of Whitby Abbey* (1779), 338–40.

6   R. Lidster, *The Scarborough & Whitby Railway*, Centenary Volume (1985).

7   Daysh, *op. cit.*, 18, 20, 24.

8   A. Clifton Taylor, *Another Six English Towns* (1984), 62–3.

9   T. H. English, *An Introduction to the Collecting and History of Whitby Prints*, 2 vols. (1931).

10   H. M. Colvin, *A Biographical Dictionary of British Architects* (1978), 634.

11   J. Davison & G. Leach, 'Whitby Commercial Newsroom', *Whitby Literary & Philosophical Society Annual Report* (1975), 15.

12   *The Whitby Magazine*, I (1827), 226–7.

13   M. Girouard, *Town and Country* (1991), 70.

14   Colvin, *op. cit.*, 192.

15   Ibid., 441–2; *Whitby Magazine*, I (1827), 226.

16   Colvin, *op. cit.*, 521–2; A. Taylor, 'William Lindley of Doncaster', *Georgian Group Journal* (1994), 30–42.

17   Colvin, *op. cit.*, 768–9.

18   Ibid., 76.

19   *The Universal British Directory* (1798).

20 E. Baines, *History, Directory & Gazetteer of the County of York*, 2 (1823).

21 N. Vickers, *A Yorkshire Town of the Eighteenth Century; Probate Inventories of Whitby, North Yorkshire 1700–1800* (1986), 85.

22 D. Cruickshank & N. Burton, *Life in the Georgian City* (1990), 106–10.

23 Ibid., 137–49.

24 Clifton Taylor, *op. cit.*, pl. 38.

25 G. Young, *A History of Whitby*, 2 (1817), 511n.

26 White, *op. cit.*, 121.

27 D. Butler, *Summer Houses of Kendal* (1982).

28 Cruickshank & Burton, *op. cit.*, 190–205; R. D. Bell, 'The Discovery of a Buried Georgian Garden at Bath', *Garden History*, 18, i (1990), 1–21.

29 Vickers, *op. cit.*

30 Girouard, *op. cit.*, 72.

31 *Whitby Magazine*, I (1827), 226–7.

32 Davison & Leach, *op. cit.*, 14–19.

33 *Victoria County History; Yorkshire North Riding*, 2 (1923), 523.

34 Charlton, *op. cit.*, 344.

35 R. T. Gaskin, *The Old Seaport of Whitby* (1909), 373.

36 J. M. Freeman, *W. D. Caroë; His Architectural Achievemen*t (1990).

37 *Whitby Magazine*, I (1827), 243–4, 267–9, 303–6, 337–9, 361–4.

38 N. Curnock (ed.), *The Journal of John Wesley,* most accessibly quoted in A. Whitworth, *Whitby As They Saw It* (1991), 15.

39 Colvin, *op. cit.*, 634; Girouard, *op. cit.*, 71–2.

40 *Whitby Gazette*, 28 December 1861.

41 Colvin, *op. cit.*, 734.

42 G. Young, *A Picture of Whitby*, 2nd ed. (1840), 186.

43 *Gentleman's Magazine*, LVIII (1788), 69–70.

44 Charlton, *op. cit.*, 340.

45 Young (1817) *op. cit.*, 944.

46   *Ibid.*, 944.

47   *Ibid.*, 558; J. Tindale, 'The Campion Factory and Campionville', *Whitby Literary & Philosophical Society Annual Report* (1993), 12–16.

48   Young (1817) *op. cit.*, 505; Young (1840) *op. cit.*, 164.

49   Young (1817) *op. cit.*, 944.

50   It is often attributed to Jarvis Coates, Benjamin's father, but that seems too early for its style, while Benjamin is shown by his will (Borthwick Inst., Cleveland D. Mar. 1757) to have been a very wealthy man; White, *op. cit.*, 66.

51   At that time a set of hemispherical bells was removed (they are now fixed in the gallery). Pile, *op. cit.*, shows the cupola as it was in 1956. N. Pevsner, *The Buildings of England; Yorkshire, The North Riding* (1966), 366, dates the chancel and apse to 1890, but an apse certainly existed before 1852 (OS 60" Map).

52   DoE List of Buildings of Special Architectural or Historical Interest, Urban District of Whitby (1972); NMR Library Buildings Files.

53   Pevsner, *op. cit.*, 396.

54   Young (1817) *op. cit.*, 558.

55   Girouard, *op. cit.*, 70, pl. 51; Young (1817) *op. cit.*, 511, oddly describes this house as being 'after the plan of the Mansion House in London'. See also P. Burnett, 'Old Whitby: The Mansion House, Flowergate', *Whitby Naturalists' Club*, 10 (1945–7), 15–19.

56   Young (1817) *op. cit.*, 944.

57   A. Byrne, *London's Georgian Houses* (1986), 154.

58   Charlton, *op. cit.*, 340; estate agents' particulars for 'Lynden Gate'.

59   White, *op. cit.*, 61.

60   Girouard, *op. cit.*, 70, pl. 50; M. Keighley, *Whitby Writers – Writers of Whitby and District 1867–1949* (1957), 225.

61   Davison & Leach, *op. cit.*

62   Young (1817) *op. cit.*, 589–90.

63   Copy in Whitby Museum.

64   Baines, *op. cit.*

65   *Whitby Magazine*, I (1827).

66   Charlton, *op. cit.*, 340.

67   P. Shaw Jeffrey, *Whitby Lore and Legend* (1952), 9.
      There has been some confusion between this house
      and Spring Cottage, which survives. Both are marked
      on Wood's map of 1828.

68   C. Waters, *Whitby: A Pictorial History* (1992), pl. 131.

69   Clifton Taylor, *op. cit.*, 62–3.

70   Wood's map of 1828.

71   H. Belcher, *Illustrations of the Scenery on the Line of
      the Whitby & Pickering Railway* (1836), 19; K. Hoole,
      North-Eastern Branch Line Termini (1985), 158;
      White, *op. cit.*, pl. 73, show this intriguing building
      in use, disuse and collapse.

72   Lidster, *op. cit.*

73   It seems to be this house which is portrayed in the
      curious painting illustrated in J. Tindale, *Fishing out
      of Whitby* (1987), 16.

74   Pile, *op. cit.*

75   Young (1817) *op. cit.*, opp. 512.

76   Pevsner, *op. cit.*, 260–1; Colvin, *op. cit.*, 76, 768–9.

77   Young (1840) *op. cit.,* pl. opp. 256.

78   D. A. Spratt & B. J. D. Harrison, *The North York
      Moors; Landscape Heritage* (1989), 146, pl. 23.

Index

For a complete list of
Keele University Press and Ryburn
books in print, please write to
Keele University Press, Keele University,
Staffordshire ST5 5BG, England